I0390979

STEP INTO VISIBILITY WITH VIDEO

a call to empower entrepreneurs

written by

MICHELLE LEWIS

ISBN: 1541269756
ISBN-13: 978-1541269750

DEDICATION

To every single woman who is looking to start their journey in visibility. To stop believing the lies they were force-fed as children. To create a different reality. To be willing to give it the guts and bravery to actually "try".

You, my dear, are my hero.

CONTENTS

ACKNOWLEDGMENTS

Much of what I've learned has come from a steady uphill battle since childhood.
These visibility-enhancing techniques are a divine accumulation of the wisdom of my Parents, Morning: Spirit: Wolf, Joe Dispenza, Dr. Stephen Ward, Priscilla Shirer and my Creator that have revealed themselves to me throughout the years.
Thank you to each and every one of you for your patience and grit.

1 THE BIGGEST LIE

Have you been brainwashed into believing you have nothing valuable to offer?

If I were your enemy, I'd slowly, gradually, whisper lies about you into your ear until you were convinced that the whispers *were actually your own thoughts.* I'd throw dust, every day, at the diamond of your soul until it was so far buried in sand that you would forget what it looked like and only see dirt instead. I'd work hard, every day, to weave a tapestry of my reality so detailed that, as it formed around you, you'd be convinced it was yours, *your own reality*.

Have you been brainwashed into believing you have NOTHING valuable to offer?

We've all been there. Whether it's from our parents, friends, bullies, illness or trauma - we've all been convinced at some point *{usually in our childhood}* that we're really not worth much. Our romantic relationships usually validate that hypothesis, so by the time we've graduated college, we're determined our dreams won't become reality.

If you're anything like me, you had HUGE dreams. Mine started really young, where I'd fashion twine into a harness and walk my chickens around our property. Or strap palm branches on my arms and jump off things - convinced that I could fly.

That turned into wanting to be in the movies...where anything was possible. I could be a jungle explorer, a dancer, an astronaut - getting paid to make believe. That sounded incredible to me!

But then I got bullied in middle school. Told I was ugly, fat and worthless. My acting coach, who happened to be a well-known actress at the time, told me I didn't have the looks to be in front of the camera.

And I believed her.

I was presented with a reality by my bullies and my acting coach, and I accepted them as my own. I adopted someone else's truth. And it never quite fit. It was uncomfortable to wear. *The print didn't look good on me.*

- Chances are, you are wearing a reality that isn't yours, either.

Does it look like parental shame, spousal guilt, *"I'm only a Mom"* or *"I'll just work at this job until..."*?

The list goes on. And on.

- Or, maybe you've stepped into the entrepreneur space + are still struggling with getting in front of that camera.

I certainly understand that. My wounds led me down the path of being a stand in. Replacing actors when they weren't working so that sound, lighting and camera crews could use my body to get the next shot right. Get the irony? I was in front of the camera...but not when it was actually on.

Sound ridiculous to you? It absolutely was.

In your life, it may look like:

-Cringing at every photo/video you take + hitting "delete"

-editing and re-editing all of your social media posts, worried about what other people might think

-Seeing other people doing what you're trying to do...and seeing yourself as less than *{this is also known as comparisonitis}*

-Living in a pre-emptive state of defeat, meaning that you don't even really try because you already feel too discouraged to take action

-Hearing repeated thoughts trying to convince you to count yourself out

None of this is embarrassing, dear. This is our current reality and it has to be honestly looked at.

I know I've felt all of those things, and it kept me pinned down to the floor.

And there is one statement you HAVE to hear today, that you have to believe + that has to make you ANGRY.

And that is:

IT'S ALL BEEN A LIE.

Yep, you heard me right. All of the damage, pain, words, feelings, all of it...have been hellishly orchestrated to convince you that those outer perceptions of you are true. Because if you can be convinced of that, you will never ever become the person you were designed and sent here to be.

And I, for one, want to put a stop to that in your life right now.

I know you're reading this to learn how to make beautiful videos. And I could impress you all day with my background of growing up on movie sets and working on fancy shows, but can you see that, no matter what lighting, framing or technique I showed you - none of it will be of any use until you see *the true Value that YOU have to offer?*

And I didn't learn that on a film set! I learned it while lying in bed for 2 years with a failing body. Because I'd let myself give up and give in to being a victim, a failure and a fluke.

So I'm here to show you your VALUE.

And it simply can't be seen until we strip the lies away and let the true you emerge - exposed, fresh and a little raw - to the light of truth.

It's time to stop grieving over who you WISH you were and realize the incredible destiny you possess...that no one else on this earth has.

You are here for a reason.

- You are equipped. You have all the tools you'll ever need to do this.
- You are chosen. You're not a mistake. You have a distinct voice that no one else can copy.
- You are strong. You're still here - you've survived the past and it's time to create an amazing future for yourself and those you're meant to reach.
- You can do this. Every detailed aspect of "this" - your life, your business, your goals, your intentions - you can do it.

This list is a compilation of what are called "affirmations". And, frankly, there's no quicker way to re-write your brain with positive patterns. So put them on your mirror, in your car, on your forehead with sharpie -- wherever you can so that you'll see them every single day!

In our next chapter, I'm going to come alongside you to help you find your strengths. It's important to know your precise powers to help others so you can *crystallize your message.*

2. YOUR TRUE STRENGTHS

What are your strengths? Or is it easier to focus on your weaknesses?

Do you wake up energized by your potential and talents, or are you begrudgingly looking in the mirror at that extra weight, that never-ending to-do list or feeling totally dejected skimming the newsletters of your inbox of other "successful" entrepreneurs?

I've totally been there.

And some days, it can be hard to change out of our pajamas.

In the last chapter, we talked all about how we've been totally conned. Convinced to believe lies about our worth and reality that are totally untrue.

So, now that we are recovering from this case of mistaken identity, it's time to rip apart the "dome" of that old reality and build a new one!

Keep reading the affirmations I gave you in the last chapter, and now let's add something.

Let's add positioning.

So what sets apart video masters like Marie Forleo or James Wedmore? Oprah or Jimmy Fallon?

It isn't fame - because they haven't always been famous.

It isn't money - because each had to work hard for their success.

These masters are set apart because they were absolutely convinced, whatever the circumstances, of their POSITION. **Their powerful position.**

That they had a purpose. A message. A mission that was bigger than themselves.

So there was no time to lose with doubt, fear or other people's words.

THE TIME WAS NOW!

There was no time to live in a constant state of defeat.

So...what state are you living in right now?

Fear, failure, age, traumas, fatigue, anger, or just plain feeling asleep?

Are you sick of it yet?

Want to change it?

I certainly did. And the best way to stop looking backwards is to create a mission that moves us forward.

What's your mission?

That can be a hard question to answer in just a sentence, but it can be done. A lot of people in the business space call it a *"Mission Statement"*.

But instead of giving yourself a headache trying to piece it together, I want to encourage you to imagine something.

So close your eyes.

Keep them closed. Well, read this, then close your eyes and imagine it.

I want you to find yourself on an airplane. But not just any airplane, a private jet. I want you to simply observe what the inside of this plane looks like. What are the colors of the seats? The floor? Where are you sitting?

Now, look outside the window.

You're parked in front of a big convention center.

Now look at your lap. What are you wearing? Do you have a purse or briefcase? How's your hair? Are you wearing makeup?

What color are your clothes?

Now it's time to step off of the plane and approach the convention center. Look at the banner.

What kind of conference is it?

As you walk inside, someone is walking up to you. What are they saying?

Are they handing you a ticket to sit in the audience?

Are they giving you a one-sheet of the event because you're speaking?

Or are they barraging you with questions because you're leading the entire event?

Sit with yourself for a second. Feel what it feels like to be there at that conference. What that topic means to you. What it feels like to be in your purpose.

Now wake up and write everything down!

Don't leave anything out!

You were just communing with your future self.

And she doesn't have time for games. She isn't worried about what other people think or what may or may not fail. She is on a mission.

You are on a mission.

Your assignment is to list your strengths. And I want 50 of them!

Ask your friends, your spouse, your audience, put up a post online...then add a TON of your own. You know what they are...they may have just been forgotten over time. But we'll find them.

Do you remember my dirt analogy from the last chapter? How, if I were your enemy, I'd throw dust, every day, at the diamond of your soul until it was so far buried in sand that you would forget what it looked like and only see dirt instead?

It's time to shovel away that dirt.

Growing up, we had a few horses. And I had the pleasure of regularly going out to the corral and shoveling the manure. Even in the rain.

Raking, scooping, tossing.

It felt like a meaningless task.

But, over time, my muscles grew *{wet horse poop is heavy, by the way}*. My hands became calloused. I learned more and more about horses. How they moved, what frightened them, how they liked to be talked to. I was able to have the time to observe them, as they truly were.

We are shoveling this dirt away from your diamond, my dear.

We are observing the truth of you - in your natural, unmarred state.

And it's freaking beautiful.

Your strengths are unique, special and downright vital for our next step...which is reaching your audience with your distinct, powerful message.

So, send me your strengths, I'd love to see them!

Remember to list 50 of them. 50. For real.

Now it's time to focus on your message.

3. WHAT'S YOUR MESSAGE?

This last Thanksgiving, my family hosted the holiday at my parent's house. *I may or may not have lost a bean bag on the roof while playing corn hole with my Dad.*

About 2 weeks prior, my Mom made the calls around to see what everyone was going to bring. Someone was bringing potatoes, another a casserole, another pies, etc. Mom was going to make the turkey, despite being a vegetarian for over 20 years. Don't worry, it was good.

My point is, in order to make the dinner successful, we all had to bring different dishes to the table. And the same is true for your messaging.

Your ideal client has a lot of needs. No matter where they're at; if they're a stay at home Mom struggling with weight, a burnt out college student, a flailing solopreneur...they have a ton of needs. Needs with their business, their diet, their relationships, their mindset, their emotions. So on and so forth. And, please hear me, **you cannot and WILL not meet them all**.

They are seated at that table and it's their job to order the right dishes. The catch is, you as the expert, can only bring one dish to your client. One. *Tops.*

If your client is savvy enough to consider your "dish", you better be darn sure that their menu has a very clear description of what you're offering. *And this is where most people fail.*

Clarity is one of the hardest things to achieve in your business.

Go into any business-minded Facebook Group and you'll see tons of people pitching themselves, presenting themselves, trying to position themselves...but you'll leave confused. Because there's no specificity. There's no clarity. *There is no excellence.*

Because it takes time. It takes hard work!

It's much easier, in the beginning, to be generic.

But, when you end up drowning in brand confusion, fuzzy copywriting and zero clients...you'll start realizing how exhausting lack of clarity really is.

When you can pinpoint exactly who you are, who you serve and what you do, the words start rolling off of your tongue *{or keyboard}* like butter.

The best place to start are your Pillars.

Let's narrow down how you serve to 2 or 3 categories. And I don't mean huge, broad topics. *I mean niched down, specific, tangible things.*

If nothing comes to mind, just start jotting down all of the results you help your client achieve. Then, put them into 2 or 3 categories. Boom. You've got your business pillars!

Here's an example. If I were to call myself a Life Coach, I might make my pillars Mindset, Body and Spiritual Practices. That way, if you were to look me up online, you'd know exactly what I focus on.

Is this starting to make sense?

Let's translate your Pillars into videos.

It's easy to whip out the video camera, but usually when the record button is hit, we blank. *What on earth are we supposed to talk about?*

So, before you roll out that red carpet, you need an action plan for your content. That's where the pillars come in.

But guess what? You've already created the categories for your Youtube Channel, Instagram, Facebook or Website videos!

Isn't that handy? Your pillars are your main categories for your videos.

Now, take your Pillars + make bullet points under each category.

This is when you go into crazy detail.

So, if we're using my Life Coach example, I might list the following under my Mindset Pillar: Meditation, Affirmations, Intentions and Wake Up Calls. And I've already come up with at least 4 videos under one of my pillars.

Now, I can break that down even further.

If one of my video topics was Meditation, I can break that down into videos about specific meditation masters, how I meditate, what meditation does to the brain, etc. etc.

Now, I've got at least 16 videos under my Mindset Pillar.

Pretty cool, huh?

When we have clarity in ourselves, we have clarity in our strengths. When we have clarity in our strengths, we have clarity on our message.

And now that we've gotten clarity in our message, I'm going to show you how to spearhead your voice in your market.

To do that, we need you to show up at your best, nail your topic and have the right equipment to support you.

So, write down your Pillars, plan out your videos and I'll see you next chapter where we'll take our final step together and find your gorgeous voice!

4. SPEARHEAD YOUR VOICE

We have been through so much together already!

We've stopped listening to false realities, we've started to believe in our strengths and we've gotten clarity in our messaging.

Thank you so much for being on this journey with me and being open enough to doing the work. You'll never regret it.

Now, I want to get you started down the road of visibility. It's time to get in front of that camera and start creating gorgeous videos! *Are you ready?*

Let's start with you.

We need to make sure you are showing up at your very best.

This doesn't mean perfect, it means INTENTIONAL. So, think about your message -- then put yourself in the best space to present that message to your audience. That might be indoors or outdoors, just put some thought into your location.

- **What about clothes?**

What color would be best to communicate to your audience? If you haven't been through my Color training, I highly recommend checking it out on the website {VisibilityVixen.com}. Start becoming more purposeful in how you look. Your clothing, hair, makeup. Don't go overboard - we're not covering anything up, we're simply presenting ourselves as we would for a first date. I think our audience deserves that, don't you?

- **Next, let's look at your equipment. Are you all set up?**

You don't need a three-thousand-dollar camera, you can make great videos with your iphone. But we need to pay attention to the framing and lighting. A bad angle or poor lighting can ruin even the most action-packed video.

Also, remember your audio. Plug in a mic. And yes, they even have external mics for iphones! Good sound can cover a multitude of sins, so always invest in presenting yourself as professionally as possible.

- **Now, it's time to Record your brilliance!**

Don't stress out. The beautiful thing about recorded video is that you can shoot multiple takes. But here's the key. You're not allowed to re-watch what you just recorded. What I mean is, record the content and if you make a very visible flub, do it again. But that's it. None of this doing a take, hitting playback and staring at yourself doing the whole thing. You'll hate it, delete it, and that's no good.

So, instead, record it, check to make sure the shot, lighting and sound looks good when you're all done, then import it.

Because, the truth is, it's never going to be perfect. I've been doing this awhile and I still have yet to see a perfect video of myself. *But, it's not important to me.* Because I'm not perfect. And it's unrealistic to put that kind of pressure on myself.

As long as I do my best with my message, presentation and shot, I'm happy.

So please do the same.

5. THE NEXT STEPS

Sometimes, I wish I hadn't spent so much time in doubt and confusion. But, I have to remind myself that every trial and setback have not only aided my character, but have given me opportunities to come alongside others who have had similar struggles.

And what bigger struggle is there for women than their visibility?

I hope that you have thoroughly enjoyed this tasting of video visibility. It is a journey, but a worthwhile one. It's time to stop believing the lies our past has desperately tried to convince us of.

Because, my dear, the world needs you now more than ever.

I would absolutely love to hear how this book has impacted you, and on the next page you'll see further opportunities to connect with me. In the meantime, keep going and know I'm always your cheerleader.

CONNECT WITH MICHELLE

- **Download one of her free business training gifts:** VisibilityVixen.com/gifts

- **Download the Visibility Vixen® App:** VisibilityVixen.com/app

- **Check out her Online Courses:** MichelleCourses.com

- **Listen to the Podcast:** VisibilityVixen.com/podcast

ABOUT THE AUTHOR

Michelle Lewis is a visibility expert and podcast host who specializes in giving gorgeous vides, powerful livestreams and epic courses to launching lady entrepreneurs. Michelle helps her clients set up chic systems, brand themselves like a bada** and absolutely rock their videos through her online courses and Facebook Group *"Visibility Vixens"*.

Michelle has a film/tv background, working both in front of and behind the camera on shows like *"Paycheck"*, *"Pretty Little Liars" and "Chuck"*.

She lives in Los Angeles with her husband and protective pug {Olliver}. In her spare time she visits coffee shops, rides horses and writes music.

SOCIAL MEDIA LINKS

Website: VisibilityVixen.com

Instagram + Twitter: @visibilityvixen

Facebook Group: bit.ly/visibilityfb

Visibility Podcast: VisibilityVixen.com/podcast

.

www.ingramcontent.com/pod-product-compliance
Lightning Source LLC
Chambersburg PA
CBHW061238180526
45170CB00003B/1347